ISBN: 978-1-951667-01-6

Published by I AM Media Books, Michigan, USA

*Media to Awaken the World!*

www.iammediabooks.com

I AM Big
I AM Fancy
I AM Playful
I AM Sweet as candy
I AM Incredible
I AM Kind
I AM Awesome
Though the world pays me no mind
I AM is capital because I can be all things
My Father watches over me
I AM under His protective wings

This book is
dedicated to all
Hebrew Daughters
that fear

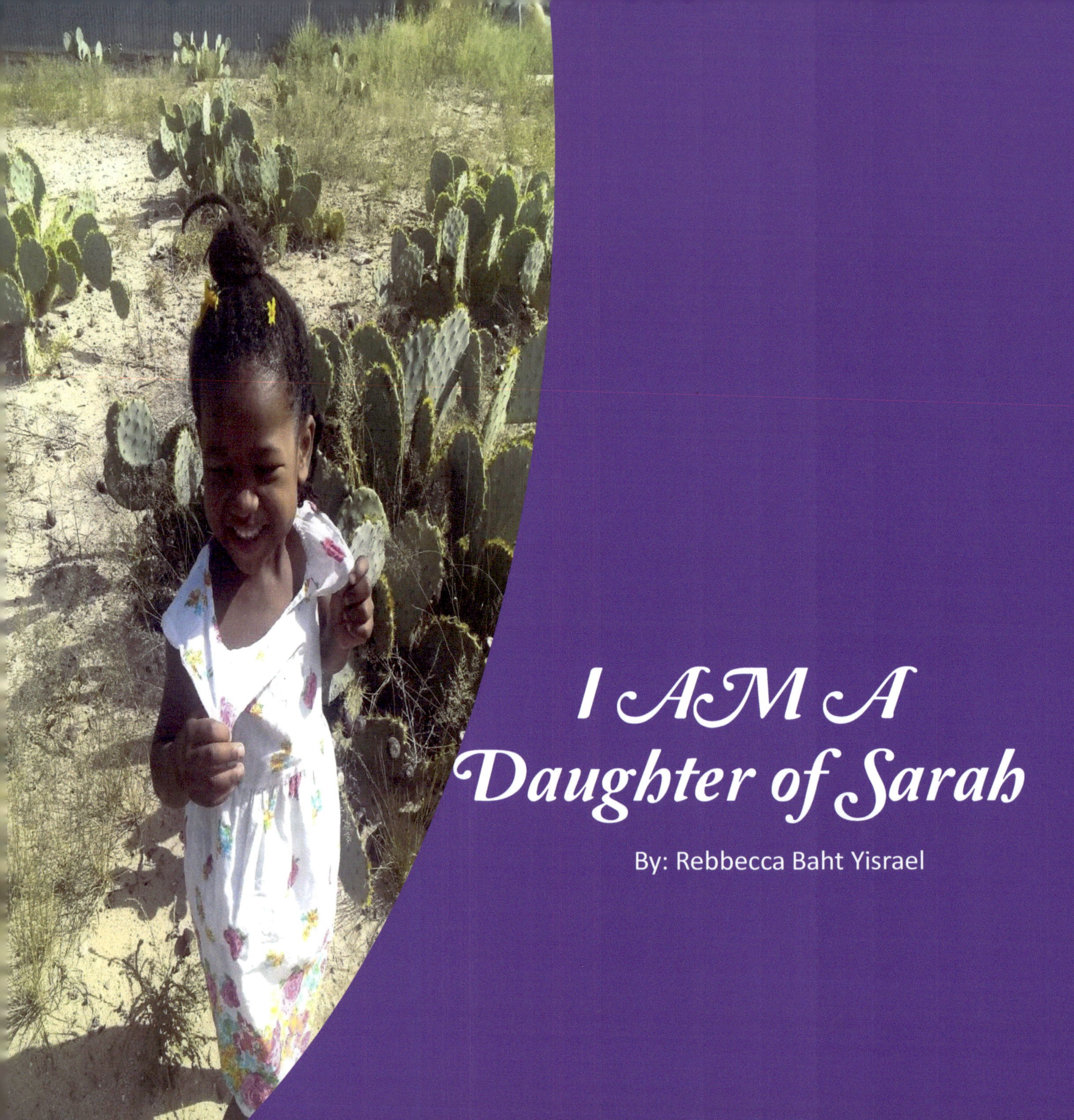

# I AM A Daughter of Sarah

By: Rebbecca Baht Yisrael

I AM beautifully made of יהוה

I will praise You,
for I am fearfully
and wonderfully
made;
Marvelous are
Your works, and
that my soul knows
very well.
Psalm 139:14

But, which is proper for women professing righteousness, with good works.
1 Timothy 2:10

I AM just the way 𐤉𐤄𐤅𐤄 made me. I AM different. I AM set apart. This is the only way to 𐤉𐤄𐤅𐤄 heart.

The world cannot comprehend the spiritual beauty 𐤉𐤄𐤅𐤄 gave me.

Before I formed you in the womb I knew you; Before you were born I sanctified you; I ordained you a prophet to the nations. Jeremiah 1:5

I AM
strong

*My Strength comes from ꓱꓵꓱꓥ.*

*In ꓱꓵꓱꓥ is my salvation and my glory; The rock of my strength, And my refuge, is in ꓱꓵꓱꓥ.*
Psalm 62:7

*I AM*
*guided*
*by* 𐤉𐤄𐤅𐤄

I may not have
earthly muscles to
lift boulders,
but יהוה gave me
armor.  I put on my
helmet of truth,
pull on my boots of
faith, grab my
shield of יהוה and
the sword of the
Word to claim
victory in the ruach.

Put on the whole armor of 𐤉𐤄𐤅𐤄, that you may be able to stand against the wiles of the devil. Ephesians 6:11

I AM
Intelligent
BIOLO
ECON
MATH
POLITICS
RELIGIO
EDUCATION

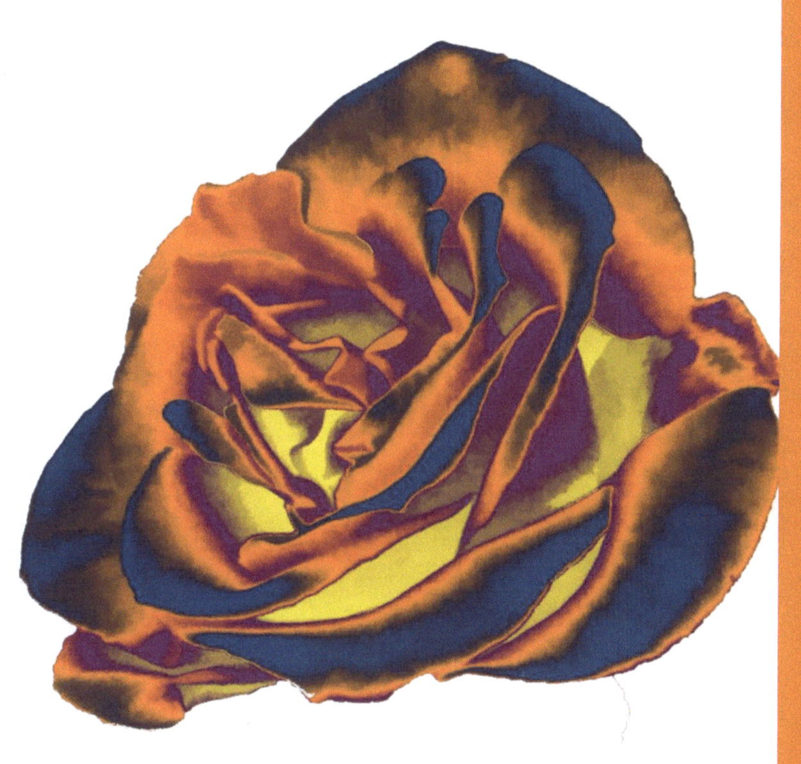

*And to man He said,
behold, the fear of 𐤉𐤄𐤅𐤄
that is wisdom, and
to depart from evil is
understanding.
Job 28:28
If any of you lacks
wisdom, let him ask
of 𐤉𐤄𐤅𐤄, who gives to
all liberally and
without reproach, and
it will be given to him.
James 1:5*

*There is only One 𐤉𐤄𐤅𐤄. Yours, O 𐤉𐤄𐤅𐤄, is the greatness, the power and the glory, the victory and the majesty; for all that is in heaven and in earth is Yours; Yours is the kingdom, O 𐤉𐤄𐤅𐤄, and You are exalted as head over all.*
*1 Chronicles 29:11*
*I will set my mind on 𐤉𐤄𐤅𐤄 and His kingdom.*

I AM wise because I honor my mother and father. Honor your father and your mother, that your days may be long upon the land which 𐤉𐤄𐤅𐤄 your Elohim is giving you. Exodus 20:12

I AM Humble

Blessed are the meek: for
they shall inherit the earth.
Matthew 5:5

I AM a child of
ЯꞀꞀV

But as many as received Him, to them He gave the right to become children of 𐤉𐤄𐤅𐤄, to those who believe in His name: who were born, not of blood, nor of the will of the flesh, nor of the will of man, but of 𐤉𐤄𐤅𐤄.
John 1:12–13
Let us hear the conclusion of the whole matter: fear 𐤉𐤄𐤅𐤄, and keep his commandments: for this is the whole duty of man. Ecclesiastes 12:13

I AM an
heiress.

With 𐤉𐤄𐤅𐤄
as my
Father, the
kingdom of
Jerusalem
is my
inheritance.

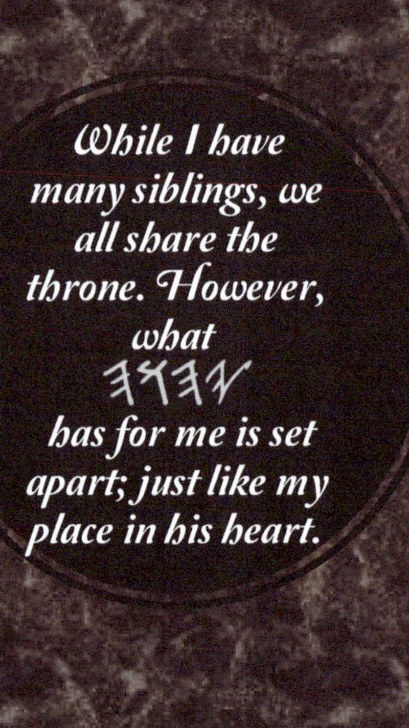

While I have
many siblings, we
all share the
throne. However,
what
NENE
has for me is set
apart; just like my
place in his heart.

I AM loved and blessed.
But seek first the kingdom
of יהוה and His
righteousness, and all these
things shall be added to you.
Therefore do not worry about
tomorrow, for tomorrow will
worry about its own things.
Sufficient for the day is its own
trouble.
Matthew 6:33–34

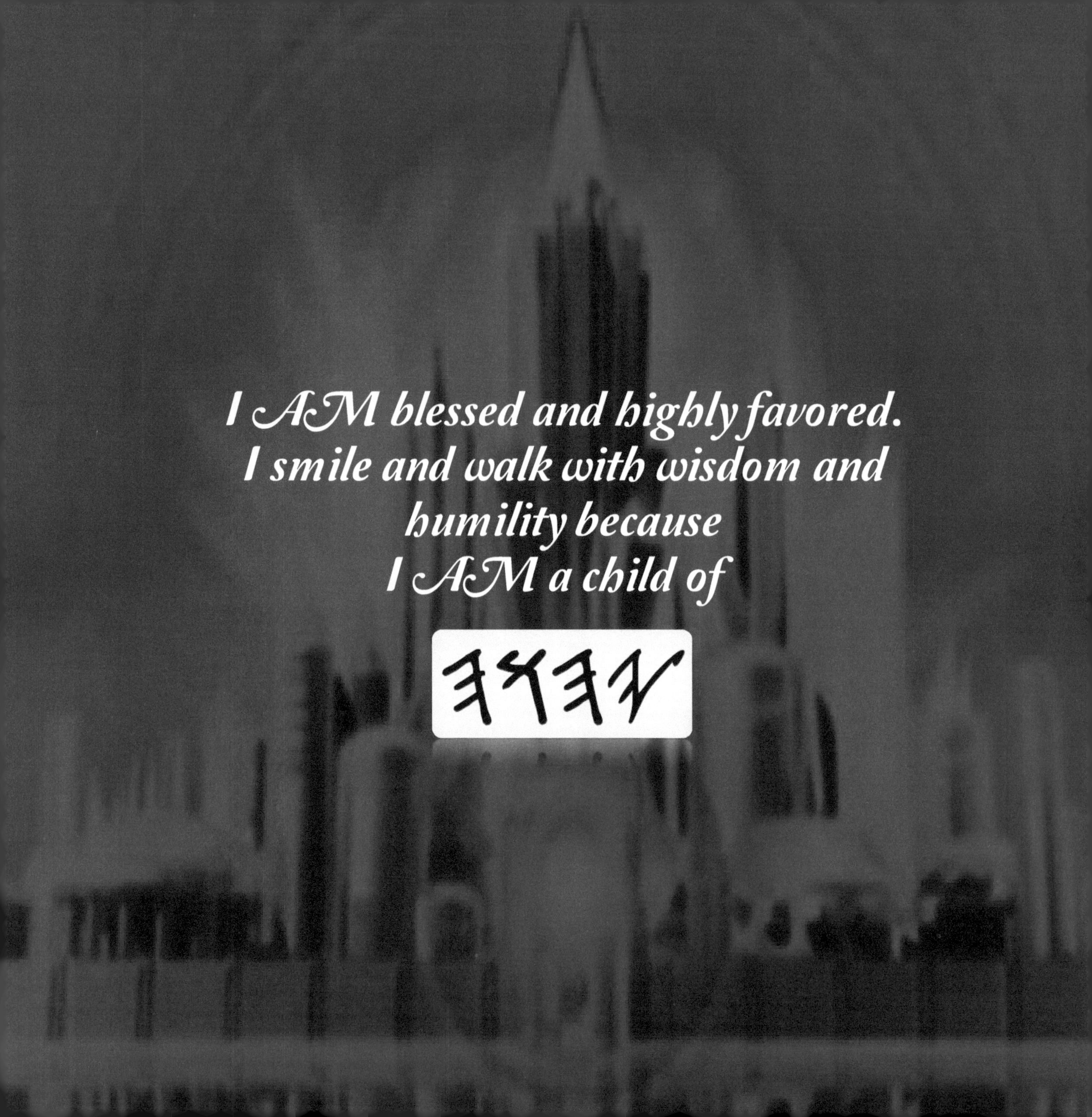

I AM blessed and highly favored.
I smile and walk with wisdom and
humility because
I AM a child of

יהוה

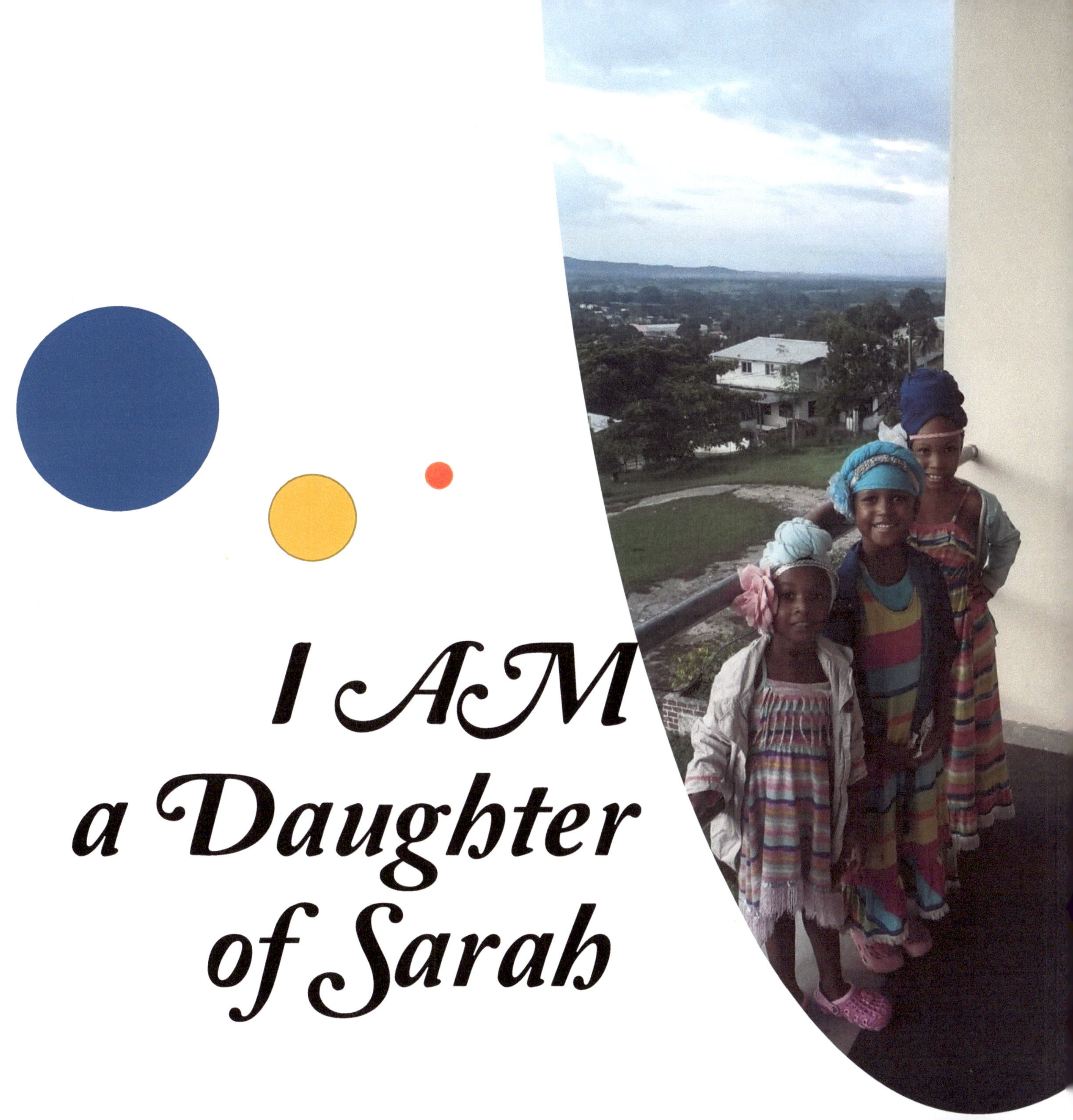
I AM
a Daughter
of Sarah

# *Additional verses and inspiration*

- *I thank 𐤉𐤄𐤅𐤄 for making me  a reflection of His love and grace and faith.  When I look at myself each day, I say "Shalom blessed daughter of Zion" and "Boker Tov beautiful daughter of Sarah"*

- *Cause me to hear Your lovingkindness in the morning, for in You do I trust; Cause me to know the way in which I should walk, for I lift up my soul to You.  Psalm 143:8*

- *Leaning on his strength gives me the victory. I AM without fear of trials that come because 𐤉𐤄𐤅𐤄 gives me strength and wisdom.*

- *Tests and trials help strengthen my patience.*

- *My brethren, count it all joy when you fall into various trials, knowing that the testing of your faith produces patience. James 1:3-4*

- *This is the book of the generations of Adam. In the day that  𐤉𐤄𐤅𐤄 created man, in the likeness of 𐤉𐤄𐤅𐤄 made he him; Genesis 5:1*

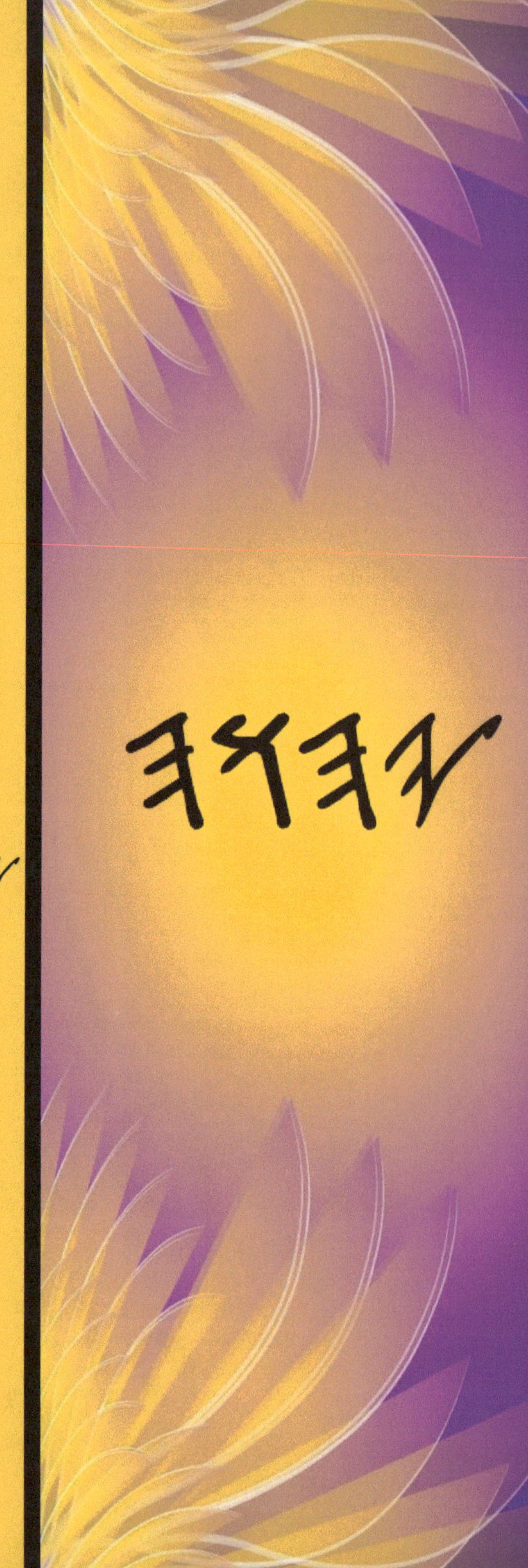